BIRD ORNAMENTS

Bird Ornaments

Angel T. Dionne

BROKEN TRIBE PRESS

Bird Ornaments
Copyright © 2025 Angel T. Dionne
First Edition

Paperback ISBN: 978-1-965412-02-2

Cover art by Jacob Arms

Published by Broken Tribe Press
Lawrence Landing Company
Raleigh, North Carolina 27609
USA, North America

Broken Tribe Press is a proud member of:

Independent Book Publishers Association
 and
Community of Literary Magazines and Presses

www.brokentribepress.com

BROKEN TRIBE PRESS

PRAISE for *Bird Ornaments*

In Angel Dionne's new book, *Bird Ornaments*, we see the world in different, dazzling parts, which don't add up into something we can immediately grasp. Her poems are surrealist because they elevate, turn, and collapse the world into a kaleidoscopic dream that reverberates through "this glass prison." "The alphabet sings to her" and, unafraid, she sings right back. Listen to "A whole river grows from [her] mouth." Listen to the vowels and consonants, verbs, and nouns, of this oracular poet as "she parts the sea with her tongue."

> – John Yau, winner of the American Book Award
> and author of *Corpse and Mirror*

Bird Ornaments achieves a masterful balance between surprising surrealist imagery and a hyper-focus on the language of the body. The collection features a powerful range of poetry, from reflective vignettes like the title track, to "A Fairy Tale for Children" (not for children), to the ruthlessly poignant maxims of "Life Cycles." A strong recommendation for fans of Jennifer O'Grady.

> – Peter Medeiros, author of
> *Deeply Gravely Quite Anxiously Concerned*

In her book *Bird Ornaments*, Angel Dionne creates surreal vignettes of human states by employing unusual metaphors, reification, and satirical language to provoke the reader to see experience from a different perspective. Her poems provide us with alternative insights to understand our own identity in today's world...

> – Laurence Hutchman, author of
> *Swimming Toward the Sun*

FOR CLAUDETTE

Contents

Inherited Maladies

This body is a dimensional graph
of genetic variations –
a head birthing dementia,
manic calamities symmetrical across time,
errant fingers knitting rheumatoid arthritis,
shingled forearms scaled by distress.

We all run perpendicular to each other.

Broken Silk

Which way did my neck bend
        before it broke?
Did it grow crooked
        with the weight of my silk?
Did it spin hot and gurgling
        down my spine?

I suck plump aphids
        from the audience's crescendo.
In the open space, I evaporate,
        hanging there like a mosaic.

Grandmother's Geraniums

My grandmother's rocking chair
breeds anguished blooms.
My hopeless geraniums, she calls them.

They blossom elsewhere, too,
in whispered secrets,
in an egg cracked too soon,
on the surface
of my grandfather's gout toe.

She often picks them
and places them in the kitchen –
forming a trail of dirt from chair to table,
a path of discarded treasures,
and earthworms
wriggling
on ugly linoleum.

Ten Surrealist Short Stories

1. My tree-trunk limbs
   send their regards.
   Insincere.
   But who am I to judge?

2. A hurriedly triaged kidney
   swells shut against the world.
   It will die next Tuesday.
   Funeral is on Friday.
   In lieu of flowers,
   bring donations.

3. My neighbour left a basket
   of headless mice at my door.
   Weeds emerge
   from their bloodied necks.
   I donate them to the needy
   and receive an award from the mayor.

4. In the dried-out timber
   lives a woman who bakes pies
   made from grass and soil.
   During winter, she stores them
   between her legs.

5. My aunt always said
   that storm drains tell the best stories.
   When rain comes, they speak.
   I've just never bothered
   to learn their language.

6. Brick by brick,
   I build my mauve indignation.
   Puffs of smoke rise from my fingers –
   the *tap-tap-tap*
   of violet incense.

7. Stains are sentient riddles
   yet to be decrypted.
   Have you ever met
   a divine splatter?
   I've been told they exist.
   Old folktale, possibly.

8. I once visited my fat cousin in Idaho.
   His wheels groaned
   against earth.
   He showed me how to gather
   a stockpile of aquatic animals
   and we sold it
   for a handsome profit.

9. They say this skeleton
   is a masterpiece
   a heap of characters
   built into a dam
   in my right ovary.

10. Frank tried to sever the link between his desire
    and stigma,
    but his stomach
    had other plans.
    We don't know what happened to him
    after he left the buffet line.

A Lesson in Morality

Parakeet your silly little worries.
Table your speech,
it's useless, at any rate.

Lobotomize your loins
and calligraph
your simple fetishes.
The dusty top shelf
welcomes them.

Candle your intrusive thoughts
in search of parasites.
Frame your wonton ideas.
Wheel your rubber arguments
down the street
like a child's bicycle.

Tourniquet your tongue –
a ghostly limb
that tastes only
the bitter sky.

Bird Ornaments

A number of vagrant, bobbled bits
bedazzle the branches
of my arteries.

Night locks the birds in the sky,
and my bones ache
in an unreachable place.

I marvel painfully
at the beating wings
and stale talons
suspended in the craggy maw
of this glass prison.

Don't you wonder
about the souls
that hung them there?

How to Sit Still

Nothing moves faster
than vowels on a bookshelf
arranged according
to size and colour.

Nothing moves faster,
than tender palms
and thin-skinned yearnings
perched between parted thighs.

Nothing moves faster,
than a withering animal
presented with
an open door.

City Living

These birds are tethered with lace.
They're dangling Christmas tchotchkes,
trinkets summersaulting
above the desperate beggars
who stew their miseries
in deep pots.

This city only lives
in the cracks of its own sidewalks --
only stretches
in the thin, white ice
of December sunlight.

The elderly woman
in the tenement building across the street
replicates her nightmares
and clothespins them to the line
to dry overnight.

In the alleyway,
a vulgar dog
comprised of wormwood and song
finds an unnamed fetus
and claims it as his own.

These streets only breathe for a moment,
in this instant,
in the echoes
of a suspended starling's
strangled chatter.

Reasons Why

Because your eyes
are ripe apricots;
although your mouth
is a pocket.

Due to the shifting feathers
atop your arms;
unless you travel the world
in a pistachio shell.

Since you once planted a seed
in a white rabbit's right ear;
despite our mother's
lemon tablecloth.

For the reason that a disco
plays in your belly;
ignoring the clatter
of last night's dishes.

By virtue of a creature
small and fluttering;
even though
you've eradicated the sparrows.

Only the past is set in stone.

What You Are

You swing oddly in my mind
with fire irises at your feet,
and the shimmer of your peacock eyes
in my hands.

You're an onyx stone catching a peculiar sunray.

You're beatified fruits,
kumquats and apples,
picked up at the local farmer's market
on Saturday morning.

You're a keepsake I've forgotten in my pants pocket.

You're the juxtaposition of the angles
at which you dance
like a ghost set askew
by an uncertain breeze.

You're an old signpost crooked in the dirt.

You're the chrysalis tones
I hear in your voice,
the rain and the murmur
of an unfed pigeon.

You're the tang of sheep sorrel –
piscean summer offering.

I straighten you out, but you always fall back.

Childhood

When I was a child,
I was a faded door.

My father tried to patch me up
with sanding paper,
white paint, new hinges
that rusted in the summer rain.

When I was a child,
I was textured fabric.

Rough and grating
webbing
against my mother's fingers,
moth-eaten
at the back of the closet.

When I was a child,
I was a screen window.

Catching flies sticky with heat --
and a sickly
aluminum scent.

When I was a child,
I was a downed fledgling.

I was broken-necked jerking
on the hot asphalt
before the sad shudder of death.

Emergency Flare

I wrote you a message – sent by telegram.
I pray you've noticed
how I've wrapped liquid
around the moon for you.
How I've glued a lovebird's wings
to the past's
fading body.

I perform a barefooted ballet for you,
my swirling dance
an emergency flare.
My chest breeds distress signals
but you always
avert your eyes.

My Neighbor's Yard in Summer

An ornament breaks
and becomes the sun,
gleeful glimmer of light,
tint of tender Neptune.

A decapitated robin
beneath the backyard shed
quickly evolves
into something more
than a question.

Bastard Equation

A fortnight,
a week,
and a day,
equal my mother's disillusionment
divided only by the years it takes
to properly birth
a diminished function.

We arrive
at the price of my ego.

Add a dozen unfulfilled desires
to hear the truth
of my mother's pains.

They only burrow
as far down as her bones.

Card Game

Pick up the final verse,
already dead
and tucked away.

The spades and Kings
scatter
into daybreak.

But you already knew
that penance
weakens all
but the strongest.

Taunting

A fist of blackened coal
throbs like the ocean
and empties my head of consonants
in a terrible way.

In their place, proper nouns,
reflect a lonely mirage
meant only for me.

Later,
a pheasant deposits an apple core
in my bed.
I try to ignore it as daylight arrives
with the scent of bergamot --
silver,
like a Holy medallion.

By midday,
the sun ridicules the earth,
and I abuse it in a mocking tone
until I, too, am redeemed.

Bird Selection

A man in a songbird suit
roosts
on the electrical wires
outside my window.

He gathers with the crows,
forming a burdened congregation --
a collection of lice-infested plumage
and taffy beaks.

The horizon shakes
a discordant concept,
and I am given the impression
that this small progress
is what matters most.

Elite Lamprey

Starved elite rattle,
      clack,
clatter their bones
      in shadowed frolic.

They swaddle greedy algorithms in shrink wrap
      and *tick* time away
with the *tick-tick-tick*
      of unkept, unkempt promises.

A feeding frenzy of vultures,
      reproducing scavenger hysteria,
sculpting a parasitic lamprey,
      that gorges on tepid flesh
and the aspirations of the masses.

A Tale of Infestation

Gnathonemus Petersii
carefully crafted from sea glass
and fungal kelp,
lives underneath my ragged fingernail.

It smells of moldy shoes
and corruption.

Resisting the urge
to peel it like a scab
proves more difficult
than I thought.

The weakly electric fish writhes a joyful tremor,
navigating the muscles with ease.

It prances about the metacarpals
and sore phalanges.
My skin quickens;
joints swell and ache.

At night, I pray over it
although I am not devout.

When my finger begins to exude
yellowed pus,
I am left to prostrate myself
in uncertainty.

A funeral begins in my throat.
I weep.

I cover the mirrors in black cloth,
tearing at my arms
until they bleed –
senseless alms.

Before long,
my hands metamorphose.

They erupt into a shoal
of argent bream,
playing a child's game of cat's cradle
with the lines they have crossed.

Anatomical Transitions

This sorrow is an ineffective bowel
scrubbed clean of pleasantries.

>Penniless.
>Destitute.

This sorrow is an inflamed duodenum,
small intestine of fire,
jejunum of sparked tinder.

>Fretful.
>Trembling.

This sorrow is my left hand,
an unearthed, ancient relic.

>Rectified.
>Cleansed.

Puzzle Market

The fishmonger never sells them whole.
A puzzle, he calls them.
I'm coaxed into believing him.

I purchase the various components,
one-by-one,
until money runs out.
I collect IOUs like old receipts.

An eye, then two,
an enlarged cerebellum on sale for Black Friday.
an elongated schnauzenorgan,
$300 -- a real rarity.

The swim bladder,
auditory vesicle,
and the lagena –
a small fortune spent.

I bring the pieces home
in a knotted bag of water,
and stow them
beneath my bed.

Someday, I'll weave them together
with a needle and red twine

I'll stitch the parts into a sum,
place it into a bowl,
and tell it the story of its birth.

Relevant Options

I'd much prefer to be dynamic
with sweet tomatoes burgeoning
from the cracks
between my teeth.

I'd much prefer to be bestowed
with a transparent stasis
arousing
my magnetic fields.

I'd much prefer for a conspicuous rumbling
to move me,
to propel
my marionette-legs forward.

I'd much prefer for a magician
to wave his wand at my head
until it is transfigured
into a busy train station.

I'd much prefer to be a sculpture
of furrowed candle wax
so that I can melt
in the heat of your flame.

French Pawnshop

I've sold my fair share
of briny notions.
A *sombre* freeze-dried prawn collection
hollows
my cocoon husk.

I am only *un petit objet*,
a cherrystone crustacean
left on the mantle. Family heirloom.

This hoard is only a symbol.

Diminuitive *bibelots*
frame the foundation
of my faith.

Dictionary of Synonyms

A synonym for life is a quail egg,
a frozen bud,
an implanted memory,
a fractured branch,
weighed down
by good intentions.

A synonym for death is a continent afloat,
a shoeprint
in wet cement,
an obelisk
trained to run.

A synonym for sleep is a tired mule,
a limping calf slaughtered,
with merely a word
paused between us.

Borges Story

The roof leaks abandoned suspicion,
and torn wood fragments
are lodged in the sunrise,
paralyzing tomorrow's breath.

My feet disintegrate
into the daggered floors,
a signal
for the jaded.

A bear's den of question marks
and explanations
is scrawled
on the soles of my feet.

My legs have always been a Borges story –
a garden of forking paths,
a book of sand,
a library of babble,
burbling commitments.

Drunk's Burden

The drunk's burden
is his barstool,
held together by crooked phrases
and songs
that nudge one to remember
the blades of gentle lessons.

Night leaks nostalgia –
a theory without proof.
Where is the substance?
His wearied allegories
spin no tales here.

When the bar closes,
he fashions a lamppost --
a rudimentary construct
featuring silhouettes
and dank fever.

A syllable
rides on his back,
thick
with his brandied breath.

Formal Logic of Vagrants

If the stars decompose
to form a cacophony of vagrants,
then patience is fleeting.

If fleeting patience is in its solid state,
then we've managed
to interpret the proof.

Therefore, we've only just begun
to anesthetize our riddles
before slicing them
from gullet to tail.

A Comedy for the Tragic

The scene reveals a muddy riverbank
and a gossamer river
flows smoothly downstage.

From above, a spotlight moon
illuminates a putrefying bird.

Cue laugh-track.
The audience titters.

This bird has been washed ashore.
and rests upon a lymphatic canvas
of silt and mud.

The audience knows that come morning,
it will be consumed by insects.

The audience coos
like a flock of pigeons.

The swollen carcass inches forward,
bloated,
its open eyes
cast toward the audience
in humiliation.

Acknowledging the languid corpse,
the river bleats
an injured sheep.

The spotlight goes out.

Intermission.

When curtains open,
the river gently licks the tip
of the bird's chipped beak
which opens slightly
and vomits a series
of white eggs.

There they hatch,
in damp clay.

The mating ritual is complete.
An orchestral symphony begins,
and the spotlight now shines a solemn light
on the empty riverbank.

The curtains close. The audience claps.

The Minister's Query

I disassemble the clumsy calculation
that the minister
has scribbled on the wall with white chalk.
He licks his fingers
as though that's the answer.

I ponder his mistake,
thrust the numbers
between my back molars,
and spit out
a decipherable calamity.

In the end,
I plant the square root
in a terra cotta pot,
and grow the answers
on my back porch.

True or False

True and false
are the same bird.

They're fading fatalities
and thinly-veiled threats.

I dreamed up stone
and polished it
to ward off this hex.

But the only answer was to braid
the threads of a tired life
into a useful object.

One day,
things will change.

Diagram of an Argument

I argue that drunkenness
is self-induced longevity,
and that there are
many shades
of desire.

My mother deduces
that womanhood tastes
like pondwater,
and sometimes
fresh pine sap.

She holds her tongue in her mouth
like a drastic medicine
and later sets it
on her finest China.

Much can be inferred
from this necessary act.

Accordingly,
a woman thinks in different degrees
of progressive blindness.

Keen Observations

A sealed envelope
contains ten dirty letters
all disordered.

A panting cat
drags an apple orchard
down the street.

In a dirty tenement window
I see remnants --
a patchwork quilt of regret.

Mother Made Us

Mother made us into birds,
he admits.
His mouth is a portal,
a door slightly ajar.

Mother walks through it.

Her steps sound like milk,
my brother says.

He spits her out,
chewed,
her heels resembling
a horrible,
masticated mess.

Mother unravels at our feet --
a puddle
of muted gold.

Exhibit of Tooth Decay

A haphazard exhibit
displays broken teeth
in glass containers, and
dislocated jaws,
with bones
eaten away by radium paint.

I pay the $5 admissions fee
if only to stand in awe
of something
greater than myself.

A Fairy Tale for Children

In a strange little house made of tin, a woman named Grandmother lost her arms at the age of seventy-three. She had no children. It was a day like any other day when she woke to find that her arms had been replaced by giant string beans. She asked her husband, Grandfather, if he'd done it. He was prone to pranks of all sorts, after all.

This is very odd, he said. *But I had nothing to do with it.*

He poked at her with his egg yolk crusted breakfast fork. Poke. Poke. Grandmother flinched.

Despite her swinging string bean arms, she did not feel any different. Still, Grandfather figured they ought to call the doctor, whose last name was, well, Doctor.

Dr. Doctor arrived an hour later wearing his caterpillar eyebrows and pussy-willow mustache.

How do you keep them from turning into butterflies? asked Grandmother, tapping the tip of his mustache. It wriggled at her touch, and Grandmother giggled. Grandfather cast a disapproving glance her way.

Vaseline, and plenty of it, replied Dr. Doctor.

Grandfather scoffed.

Dr. Doctor listened carefully to her heavy heart, checked the rawness of her throat with his penlight, and investigated her waxy ears. Then, he licked his thumbs, and smoothed his caterpillars down with spit.

Everything seems to be in order, he declared.

But what about my arms?

Grandmother raised her string beans as high as they could go, which wasn't very high at all. He took hold of one and weighed it in his large hands.

Firm and fresh. I would just leave them be. These things have a way of working themselves out.

He gave Grandmother a barbiturate and prescribed a glass of whiskey at bedtime. He told her to have two if one didn't help. Grandmother soon adapted to her legumes and learned all sorts of things. She learned how to grasp a pen, how to wrap her string beans around Grandfather's avian shoulders, how to clear the table with just one swift swipe.

Woman's work, Grandfather said.

He still did his part, though. Every morning, he misted her along with the ferns in the sunroom. She took great joy in standing amongst the potted plants. Sometimes, he spread a thin layer of his own manure around her bare feet, to keep her string beans green and crisp.

Grandmother and Grandfather even joined the neighbourhood children in their summer games. Her arms had become popular playthings. *Jump beans*, the children called them. They'd swing Grandmother's floppy arms around and around. All day long, they would laugh and play and eat the silken summer sun until it dribbled down their pointed chins. It was around this time that a little girl with burnt-orange hair and an upturned, porcine nose asked to join in on their games.

Of course, they all replied.

But the girl wasn't all that skilled at jump bean, and when another child tried to take over, the orange little girl cried and cried until the gutters ran with her tears and flooded the neighbour's basement. So, they allowed her to continue.

Faster, faster, she told Grandmother.

Faster and faster, Grandmother swung her beans. Faster. Faster still.

Thud.
Crack.
Squelch.

A junk-drawer of skull meat spilled onto the pavement.

The street cleaner came the next day and swept away the child's broken body. Grandfather hosed down the sidewalk as an orange-haired mother and father wept, placing flowers on the leftover stain.

In an act of mercy, Dr. Doctor came with his scrunched-up caterpillars. His mustache had turned to seed-carrying fluff. With Grandfather's help, he expertly sawed Grandmother's string beans off at the shoulders, slicing through the tough vegetable fibers with a surgeon's scalpel. Later, Grandmother threw them out the window and into the backyard, where a flock of grackles tore at them and carried the beans off into the sky.

A Gift from My Father

My father brought me a vacant shell
when he returned from his travels.

We split it open
with a nutcracker.

Inside, we found a vague vision
of a chicken,
a sinewy old man,
a Tetris cube painted blue,
a scroll of dead languages,
a sick primordial pouch,
a broach made of sharp stones,
his unspoken secrets – badly tainted,
and a smeared half-moon.

What will you do with them? he asked.
I still haven't
figured it out.

Waiting

She walks into
my gracious vessel
and slumbers
in the fragrant petals
of last year's gardenias.

Spent.

I am an opaque window
dressed
in underserving cobwebs.

My bland fruit,
suckling on your finger,
only glimpses
at understanding.

She sits
with her oblong limbs spread,
and her head like a grapefruit
waiting to be juiced.

The Sum of What We Are

We are wasted shells
and squandered pennies
at the tail end of a storm.

We are shrunken heads
and atrophied arms
dumped
in alleyways.

We are elegiac carapaces,
and exoskeletons
squirming
in our rightfully assigned gutters.

The Outfit I Wore to the Funeral

I stitched this red dress
from yarn
steeped in time.

A dead fish hangs
like a pendant
stitched along my throat –
 my own personal albatross.

On my feet
I wear the weary entrance
of a cavern.

My teeth scrape the ceiling
and become
worthy adversaries.

Memories That Keep Me Up at Night

A friend I once lost
walked into the ocean.
I sometimes look for her
in the sea froth washed ashore.

The way I used to see poetry
in the trees,
stanzas, like quivering pears,
drooping from the branches.

A dream I once had
of a polluted ball
and my mother crying
over its diseased surface.

She climbed atop it
and kept it warm
until it hatched.

Perfume Factory

The perfume factory where my uncle works
whines a fogged howl.

An oracle
bludgeons my roof,
frightening the mummified oaths
of those who don't know any better.

His eyes look exactly like mine.

Time ripens above our heads,
splits, and shatters.

Two years later,
the factory is demolished,
but the storage tanks
remain standing.

I often supplicate myself before them
and try to salvage
a new alternative.

Fisherman's Lament

Anthers,
cadaverous,
shiver into form – a rudimentary polymer,
from the crook of her arm,
stinking like last month's meat.

Bastard of a thought, she says.
Earnest attempt.
Hook wedged in gullet.

Odorous material
never poses questions, he warns her.
She hands him
a likely explanation
knotted in understanding –
as quiet as a virtue.

Death deals differently.
These words appear
cut into the underside
of the fisherman's white hand.

He knits her a yawn in response.

Life Cycles

This empty basin
is the earth,
civilization's cradle,
a basin
for fruit flies.

This empty basin
is my distant cousin
is a geriatric man's
spurned embryo
festering in the attic.

Instructions for Deboning a Fish

If the vertebrae whimpers
against your hesitant fingers,
demonstrate patience
in the form of a lullaby.

Cut the pectoral arch with care,
and expose an unused insult
stuck between the sharp,
alabaster ribs.

Pull the spine from its home
and claim your soulless prize.

Agonized words
only ever satisfy the dying.

This Room

This room is an old photograph
handed down to me
by my great grandparents.
I can tell the walls have been papered
with their floral discontent.

In lieu of a lightbulb
a small rodent
is wagging from the ceiling.
Its red tongue
drapes like morbid ribbon
from its snout.

This room spins a delusion
all its own;
thick water stains
utter unsettling falsehoods.

I grab a hold
of the rodent's prehensile tail
and ring its bell.

An Invitation

I've aired out the dining room
to rid it of tomorrow's ensemble –
chartreuse
gaudy
bedazzling light
from its tattered hem.

You can come over
now that it's gone.
We'll press our ears to the hardwood
and listen for the sea.

We'll make sandwiches,
and leave our dirty fingerprints
on the windowpanes –
an invitation for birds
to shimmy against the glass.

I haven't forgotten
what you once told me –
that everything
matters more than nothing,
that even the stones
beat time in their chests,
that the sea speaks
even to those
who've never set foot on its shores.

Water from Stone

The alphabet sings to her
forming a swarm
of voracious locust.

She parts the sea with her tongue,
you know,
her toes curling
just over the precipice.

Whenever she cradles
her well-meaning disasters,
I thump a conditional sentence
against a boulder --
water from stone,
finding only futile prayer.

News Report

A tweed daughter's laughter
is a dirtied gem
loved only by winter's
wanton arias.

Memories form
a smattering of galaxies.

A vinyl record
spinning across the sky
lands in British Columbia.

It doesn't make front page news.
But what do you expect?
The truth only gets you so far.

Dear Friend

Inside my friend's head
is a bundle of words
pulsing a hastened rhythm.

The smoking chimney inside her
declares a miraculous intervention,
and her voice
protests my every move.

Together,
we form a constellation,
of disconnected lamentations.

A Bribe

Pristine.
Used.

In exchange
for a rude awakening,
an awkward astonishment
propagates fowl.

Death is a welcome tool for materialists,
and a capitalist
is a beetle's mandible.

A whole river
mushrooms from my mouth.

My beige worries lead only
to useless conversation.

Records of a Life Well Lived

A fossilized stork
is a historical record of ancestry
scratching time
as if genetics were more
than heritable coincidence.

Pregnant barnacles
spill new life
into the Mariana trench's depths,
scattering souls like dry parsley,
or so I've been told.

Slowly, a rigid persona emerges
using cilia to amble
from sea
to humble mud
where it sprouts toes
and feet
and ankles –
a sort of hereditary suffering.

When a Stranger Visits

On the street,
a stranger whittles prehistoric moldings –
soft wood
crafted into antlers.

Tied around his waist
is a bloodied rabbit
dragged out of hiding by his dogs.

He stands
cradling his swollen gut,
shushing it
as though it were a hungry newborn.

Later,
I watch as a woman
feeds the bloodied rabbit
from her distended breast.

Soliciting

In the debris of bones left unclaimed,
proselytizing brochures
shred the horizon.

Have you heard the good news?
Repent now.
You can be saved.

We're all biographers
in one way or another.

The Parcel

I must
retrieve
the parcel
that fell
into my mother's lap
like
an effortless sorrow
like
a slumped ragdoll
in a box.

Home is a Place for Ghosts

My chastened voice bursts windows
and lets out the stale air;
the house exhales relief –
rancid ghost of a sigh.

In response,
a strange little man burrows
under the back porch.

His spine splinters –
crushed beneath the weight
of red soil
and spiteful expectations.

Dissecting Winter

A deer's hooves
punctuate the creeping nightshade
that flowers in the crook of my arm –
visions of a hushed
February cold.

Lonely lantern moon
dons its speckled coat,
before disappearing
into jagged, chasmal jaws.

We all murmur our own conformities,
amidst the remnants
of last winter's
desiccated branches.

The Number Four

The number Four
lines your pockets.

The number Four
deconstructs the birds,
speaks to you
in your great-grandfather's dialect,
and plants a hopeful grain
for next year's harvest.

The number Four
blots out inquiry.

The number Four
attempts the waltz,
spares your feelings,
and embalms time.

Grief is a Hat

My remorseful hand
spends a pocketful of decades,
a loose collection of days,
minutes littering
the bottom of my purse.

I pay off this debt –
this tally of skeletal birds
strung across the fence as a warning.

I wear my grief sopping wet
like a soaked hat
as though it might guard me
from yesterday's stillness.

Blood Feathers

My pelican rotates
in a carousel
of torn blood feathers
whirling like a wind-up top
on the tip of my index finger.

This plumed satellite
revolves circles
around my sun.

Please don't forget
to rewind my strings.

Entities I've Seen in Fever Dreams

A lump of masticated meat
singing opera semiseria on the sidewalk
for spare change.

        A disembodied lung
        Cosplaying as a reverend
        while the faithful throw flowers
        at its inferior lobes.

                My body transforming
                into a hardened monolith --
                an impersonable Stonehenge.
                Everyone is offended.

        My wife frying eggs
        in the palm of her hand.
        She sprinkles them with paprika
        and feeds them to the kitchen drain.

An immaterial collection
of abstract shapes --
geometric-flavoured spheres
and yonic silhouettes –
reciting haikus
until my fever breaks.

Tawdry Images

Indecent thoughts
might as well be
weekend chores,
and honey-dos,
and spring-cleaning burdens.

This collection of stripped polaroids
finds itself aroused

Nobody's counting on it,
anyway.

Banality Smells of Rotten Meat

Marinated platitudes,
fermented,
stink a fetid bouquet
on your lips.

We can all see last year's promise
lodged like spinach
between your teeth.

Depression

My latest mental breakdown
was a stationary thought,
a nestling wren earthed
way too soon.

Gravity's poor victim.

Fragmented Birth

I ate my hometown
in a fit of rage,
chewed up the town hall
and used the naked tree in the park
to pick my teeth.

My hometown tastes
like sweetbreads
like old birth
like soot.

Call me sentimental,
but I left my grandmother's house standing
and consumed the neighbour's bungalow
in its place.

My sister later wrote a poem about it
but nobody ever
takes her seriously.

Fallacies

A slippery sloped red herring
built a man
out of straw
burned him in effigy –
an offering
to appeal to authority.

Every once in a while,
I beg a loaded question.
This gambler's roulette wheel
has to stop somewhere.

Moonlit Holler

Small
crystalized
whooping
cranes
hatch
from
the
sidewalk
and
whoop
a
dead
language.
Sumerian,
maybe?

Combustion

I think of
spontaneous human combustion
the way one thinks of
Christmas morning
childhood summers
their wedding day
the birth of a firstborn son.

I can only hold out hope
for so long.

Smoked Herring

My wife has taken
to smoking herring in bed.

She says it wards off the trumpet vines
that asphyxiate her
in her sleep.

A fishy spell,
she calls it,
lighting the mandible
with a match.

The murky scent
seeps thick into her pillow
and I am astounded
by how lucidly she speaks
with dreams like cotton
white-pasted to her lips.

Night is a fickle,
beaten animal.

Holding Onto Hope

My soul is in the same damn place
as where it started --
incubating beneath a chicken
in a dirty barn.

Something has to give.

Perhaps next Tuesday
will be different.

Publication Credits

Some of the poems in this book have appeared in earlier forms in the following publications: *PISSOIRE, eYeland, Petrichor, Mormyridae, Broken Tribe Review*, and *Lucy Writer's Project*.

ABOUT THE AUTHOR

Angel T. Dionne is an associate professor of English literature at the University of Moncton Edmundston campus. She holds a PhD in creative writing from the University of Pretoria and is the founding editor of *Vroom Lit Magazine*. Her writing and art have been featured in several experimental publications.

She is the author of a full-length collection of short fiction, *Sardines* (ClarionLit, 2023) and two poetry chapbooks, *Inanimate Objects* (Bottlecap Press, 2022) and *Mormyridae* (LJMcD Communications, 2024). She is also the co-editor of *Rape Culture 101: Programming Change* (Demeter Press, 2020).

www.ingramcontent.com/pod-product-compliance
Lightning Source LLC
Chambersburg PA
CBHW030502130626
46549CB00007B/2825